SEP   2010

W9-DBG-832

Holidays—Count and Celebrate!

Ramadan
Count and Celebrate!

Fredrick L. McKissack, Jr. and Lisa Beringer McKissack

Enslow Elementary

an imprint of

Enslow Publishers, Inc.

40 Industrial Road
Box 398
Berkeley Heights, NJ 07922
USA

http://www.enslow.com

To Melodee, Jen, Beth, and Laural

Enslow Elementary, an imprint of Enslow Publishers, Inc.

Enslow Elementary® is a registered trademark of Enslow Publishers, Inc.

Library of Congress Cataloging-in-Publication Data

McKissack, Fredrick, Jr.
    Ramadan-count and celebrate! / Fredrick L. McKissack, Jr. and Lisa Beringer McKissack.
      p. cm. — (Holidays-count and celebrate!)
    Summary: "Kids count from one to ten as they learn about the history and customs of Ramadan"—Provided by publisher.
    Includes bibliographical references and index.
    ISBN-13: 978-0-7660-3100-5
    1. Ramadan—Juvenile literature. 2. Fasts and feasts—Islam—Juvenile literature. I. McKissack, Lisa Beringer. II. Title.
    BP186.4.M44 2009
    297.3'62—dc22
                         2007046809

ISBN-10: 0-7660-3100-4

Printed in the United States of America

10 9 8 7 6 5 4 3 2 1

To Our Readers: We have done our best to make sure all Internet Addresses in this book were active and appropriate when we went to press. However, the author and the publisher have no control over and assume no liability for the material available on those Internet sites or on other Web sites they may link to. Any comments or suggestions can be sent by e-mail to comments@enslow.com or to the address on the back cover.

Every effort has been made to locate all copyright holders of material used in this book. If any errors or omissions have occurred, corrections will be made in future editions of this book.

♻ Enslow Publishers, Inc., is committed to printing our books on recycled paper. The paper in every book contains 10% to 30% post-consumer waste (PCW). The cover board on the outside of each book contains 100% PCW. Our goal is to do our part to help young people and the environment too!

Illustration Credits: Associated Press, pp. 9 (top), 11, 17 (both), 28 (numbers 2, 3), 29 (number 6); © Bob Daemmrich/The Image Works, pp. 19, 29 (number 7); © Ilyas Dean/The Image Works, pp. 13, 25, 28 (number 4), 29 (number 10); Courtesy of Daydream Education, pp. 15, 28 (number 5); David Grossman/Photo Researchers, Inc., pp. 21, 23, 29 (numbers 8, 9); © 2008 Jupiterimages Corporation, p. 2; Shutterstock, pp. 5, 7, 9 (bottom), 26, 27, 28 (number 1), 30.

Cover Illustration: Associated Press

Contents

Read About Ramadan!

Holidays bring people together with family and friends. People all over the world celebrate different kinds of holidays.

People who are Muslim (MUHZ-lim) submit to the will of God. This means that they are a prayerful people who try hard to follow God. Muslims pray five times every day. During Ramadan they pray more often. They may pray anywhere. When they gather in community to pray, they go to a special building called a mosque (Mawsk). Muslims call God Allah (AH-lah). Their religion is called Islam (IS-lahm).

Ramadan (RAH-mah-dahn) is a Muslim religious holiday. Ramadan takes place in the ninth month. It lasts one lunar month. Muslims follow a calendar that is set by the moon. This is called a lunar calendar. Each month in the lunar calendar starts with a new moon. The ninth new moon of the year appears at the start of Ramadan. Ramadan ends when the next new moon appears in the sky.

Ramadan is a time of fasting, praying, and giving to the poor. Muslims do not eat from sunrise to sunset during Ramadan. When people do not eat for a long time it is called fasting.

The Qur'an (Koo-RAN) is the holy book of Islam. Muslims believe that God came to a man named Muhammad (muh-HAM-ahd). They believe that God spoke to Muhammad and revealed the Qur'an to him.

When Ramadan is over, people take part in a three-day festival called Eid al-Fitr (id-AHL-fit-er). During the party, people eat a feast. A feast is a very big meal with lots of different foods.

How many minarets does this mosque have?
One

A minaret (min-ah-RHET) is a tall, thin tower on the mosque. This mosque has **one** minaret. The person who calls Muslims to prayer stands at the top of the tower. This person is called a muezzin (myoo-EZ-in). He calls people to prayer five times a day.

The minaret is important to help the muezzin be heard. If the muezzin stood on the street, or on the roof of the mosque, he would only be heard a few blocks from the mosque. Rising high into the sky helps the voice of the muezzin spread far.

This is a mosque in the country of Morocco.

How many dates do you see?
Two

There are **two** dates. Many Muslims break the fast of Ramadan by eating dates. Dates are a fruit from the date palm tree. The date palm is a tree that makes many Muslims think about life. Dates have lots of sugar in them. People eat them fresh or dried.

The young women eating dates are breaking the fast of Ramadan. After eating, they will say prayers and celebrate the end of a month of fasting.

How many girls are reading the Qur'an?

Three

During Ramadan people celebrate that God came to Muhammad and revealed the Qur'an. Muslims read the Qur'an as a way to be closer to God. They also think about the message God gave to Muhammad and try to live their lives in more prayerful ways. These **three** girls are reading the Qur'an during the fast of Ramadan.

How many boys are praying?
Four

Prayer is important during Ramadan. These **four** boys are beginning the holiday with a prayer outdoors. People spend the month fasting, reading the Qur'an, and looking for ways to help other people. Praying during Ramadan helps people focus on God and brings people closer to living according to God's will.

1 2 3 4

13

How many pillars of Islam do Muslims follow?

Five

There are **five** pillars of Islam. Pillars are practices that people follow. One pillar is called *Shahadah* (shah-HAH-duh). Shahadah means saying you believe in God and Muhammad.

Another pillar is called *Salat* (suh-LAHT). Salat means prayer. Muslims pray to God five times every day of the year. During Ramadan they pray more often.

The third pillar is very important during Ramadan. It is called *Sawm* (sahm), which means to fast. Fasting is one way for people to think about God.

Zakat (zah-KAHT) is the fourth pillar of Islam. Zakat means to give to the poor. During Ramadan it is very important to share. In some places people give food and clothes to the poor.

The last pillar of Islam is called *Hajj* (haj). Hajj means that people go to the holy city of Mecca. Muslims are asked to go to Mecca at least once during their lives.

1 Shahadah (Faith)

To believe in no God but Allah and that Muhammad is his prophet and the messenger of Allah.

2 Salat (Prayer)

To pray five times each day:
Fajr - Before Sunrise
Zuhr - Early Afternoon
Asr - Late Afternoon
Maghrib - After Sunset
Isha - Night.

3 Sawm (Fasting)

To give up food and drink during daylight hours in the month of Ramadan.

4 Zakat (Almsgiving)

To give a share of personal wealth to help people in need and support the Muslim community.

5 Hajj (Pilgrimage)

To perform a pilgrimage to Mecca at least once in a lifetime.

How many hands with henna?

Six

During the celebration called Eid al-Fitr that follows Ramadan, women and girls often paint their hands and feet with henna (hen-UH). Henna is a reddish-brown dye that is made from the leaves of a small tree. These **six** hands show different henna patterns. Painting with henna is a sign of celebration.

How many kids celebrate Eid al-Fitr?
Seven

These **seven** kids are playing. They are celebrating the end of Ramadan, Eid al-Fitr. Some cities hold festivals and parties. This festival was in Texas. There was food, dancing, and celebrations of the Muslim faith. People of all ages and religions were invited.

2

5

7

3

4

6

19

How many women pray?
Eight

These **eight** women pray before a parade in New York City. Prayer is very important to Muslims. They pray five times a day. During Ramadan they pray even more times. When Muslims pray, they have seven points of their bodies touching the earth. The seven points are the face, two palms, two knees, and two feet. These places touch the ground when they bend down on hands and knees.

How many family members celebrate?

Nine

The **nine** people in this family celebrate Eid al-Fitr, the three-day holiday at the end of Ramadan. During this time, people break the monthlong fast. It marks the start of the new moon on the first day of the tenth month.

Eid al-Fitr is a time when family and friends celebrate. They will clean and decorate their homes. They will also give money to the poor. Children will receive gifts. Many people will also buy new clothing. All people take part in prayers of thanks on Eid al-Fitr. And then they share food together.

How many special foods do you see?
Ten

Food is an important part of the end of Ramadan. These are **ten** special dishes. When the fast is broken, people give thanks to God, pray, and share meals with family and friends. The food prepared for the family is colorful and festive. Meats, fruits, vegetables, and grains decorate the table. Some of the foods smell sweet and others taste spicy. All foods are welcomed after a month of fasting.

More Information on Ramadan

The holiday of Ramadan lasts one month. During this month, people fast, pray, and give to the poor. Muslims believe this month brings them closer to God. There are many Muslims all over the world. Most of them take part in Ramadan.

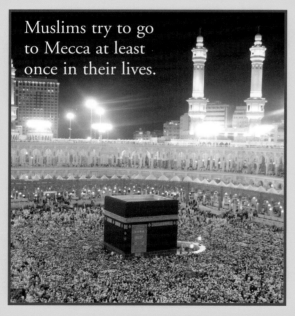

Muslims try to go to Mecca at least once in their lives.

Ramadan takes place every year in lunar month number nine. Muslims follow a lunar calendar. This means that they start a new month with each new moon. Ramadan can be on a different day every year.

During Ramadan people fast all day without food. It is hard to go all day without eating. In most places there are about fourteen hours from sunrise to sunset. When the sun goes down, people eat again. They sleep for a few hours and then eat again before the sun rises.

Ramadan is a time to share and forgive. By fasting, people think more about God and others than about their own needs. Muslims are asked to share what they have with the poor. Muslims are also asked to forgive each other for bad things they have done. They believe God wants people to share and forgive one another.

The last ten days of Ramadan are the most important. People go to the mosque to pray to God. They read the Qur'an and give to the poor. The last night of Ramadan is called the "Night of Power." This is the night Muslims believe that God showed himself to Muhammad. People spend the night in prayer, thanking God. Muslims believe God is pleased when they take part in Ramadan.

The next day, the festival of Eid al-Fitr begins. It starts with the feast that ends the fast. Muslims thank God for helping them through Ramadan. Many people show their thanks by giving gifts to the poor and also small presents to children.

Count Again!

1		One
2		Two
3		Three
4		Four
5		Five

Count Again!

6		Six
7		Seven
8		Eight
9		Nine
10		Ten

Words to Know

dates—A fruit from the date palm tree.

Eid al-Fitr—The three-day festival after Ramadan.

fast—To go a long time without food.

lunar calendar—A calendar in which the months are set by the start of each new moon.

prayer—Words said to God.

Qur'an—The holy book that Muslims read.

Learn More

Books

Douglass, Susan L. *Ramadan*. Minneapolis: Carolrhoda Books, 2004.

Gnojewski, Carol. *Ramadan: A Muslim Time of Fasting, Prayer, and Celebration*. Berkeley Heights, N.J.: Enslow Publishers, Inc., 2004.

Hughes, Monica. *My Id-al-Fitr*. Chicago, Ill.: Raintree, 2004.

Sievert, Terri. *Ramadan: Islamic Holy Month*. Mankato, Minn.: Capstone Press, 2006.

Internet Addresses

Children Activities for the Month of Ramadan
<http://www.submission.org/YES/child2.html>

Ramadan on the Net
<http://www.holidays.net/ramadan/story.htm>

Index